THE BOOMERANG

A PLAY IN ONE ACT

Melville Lovatt

TSL Drama

First published in Great Britain in 2018
By TSL Publications, Rickmansworth

Copyright © 2018 Melville Lovatt

ISBN / 978-1-912416-27-1

Image courtesy of : https://pixabay.com/en/boomerang-aboriginal-australia-wood-151561/
https://pixabay.com/en/sad-man-sad-son-loading-dock-2857248/
https://pixabay.com/en/tree-landscape-grass-nature-wood-3146731/

Rights of performance

Dedication

To my Father
Who never saw this play performed

THE BOOMERANG
A Play In One Act

was first presented as part of
the Harrow Drama Festival
by
Belmont Theatre Company
on
16 July 2000
at
The Travellers Studio Theatre, Harrow Arts Centre

with the following cast:

Ben	Jamie Noar
Grandad	Bill Baynes
Bob	Michael Collins
Doctor	Laurence Conway
Anne	Louise Carter (voice)
Directed by	Melville Lovatt

By Melville Lovatt

Full Length Plays

Small Mercies	Comedy-Drama	4M	2F
The Powers That Be	Thriller	3M	2F
Visiting Time	Family Drama	3M	2F
Desperate Measures	Dark Comedy	3M	1F

One Act Plays

Accommodation	Tragicomedy	4M	1F
The Lamp	Comedy-Drama	1M	1F
The Distressed Table	Comedy-Drama	1M	1F + Voiceover (F)
The Boomerang	Comedy-Drama	3M	1Boy + Voiceover (F)
Making Adjustments	Comedy-Drama	1M	2F
The Kiss	Thriller	2M	1F
The Weekend	Drama	2M	1F
The Grave	Drama	2M	

Duologue

Bedtime Story	Drama	1M	1F

Monologue Collections

Standing Alone (16 monologues)	Comedy-Drama	8M	8F

All enquiries to TSL Publications: www.tslbooks.uk

THE BOOMERANG

A Play In One Act

Characters

BEN	*a boy of twelve*
BOB	*a man in his early forties*
GRANDAD	*a man in his late sixties*
DOCTOR	*a man in his early forties*
ANNE	*voiceover only; early forties*

Running Time

35 minutes

Setting

The stage is divided into three areas.

__DL__, a small area with one upright wing chair.

__DR__, a small kitchen area with table, 3 chairs.
A dark tablecloth. A slice of toast on a small plate.
Table centre, two mugs.
Propped up against mugs, a white envelope addressed 'BOB'.

__Central area__, a park.
A bench UC.
Tall pine trees, suggested, off left.

In spotlight, GRANDAD *and* DOCTOR*, stand, facing each other.*

GRANDAD: Can't they operate, Doctor?

DOCTOR: I'm afraid there's no point. I'm afraid it's just too … just too far gone.

If you'd come to me earlier…

GRANDAD: How long have I got?

Pause.

How long have I got?

Pause.

DOCTOR: Six months. Maybe longer. Some people live longer.

Some people live longer … some people don't. I'm sorry.

GRANDAD: Not as sorry as me.

DOCTOR: Mr …

GRANDAD: *(Half sobs, bitterly.)* Not as sorry as me.

Blackout.

Lights Up. Kitchen. Morning.

BOB enters. He spots the white envelope on the table.

Silence.

He stares at the envelope, hesitates a moment, picks it up, opens it, reads.

ANNE'S VOICEOVER: Bob, when you read this letter, I'll be gone.

There's no real point in carrying on.

All we do is row about money all the time.

But it's not just money. We both know it's not.

I'm in a different relationship, now. I've known I'm gay for quite some time. Look after Ben. Tell him I'll write to him soon. Tell him I love him very much. Anne.

Pause.

BOB stares at the letter.

BEN enters.

BEN: When's mum coming back?

BOB: *(Quickly puts letter away.)* She's gone away, Ben. Gone away for a few days.

BEN: Where?

BOB: Auntie Pat's. Gone to Blackpool.

BEN: Why?

BOB: She needed a rest.

BEN: A rest?

BOB: She's tired. Been working too hard. She just needs a rest for a few days, right? A few days by the sea, she'll be right as rain.

BEN: Will she send us a postcard?

BOB: Might.

Pause.

BEN:	Dad …?
BOB:	What?
BEN:	Why are you and mum always shouting?
BOB:	Shouting?
BEN:	Arguing?
BOB:	Eh?
BEN:	You're always arguing.
BOB:	No. No, we're not.
BEN:	I can hear you.
BOB:	Listen, Ben. Listen, now look, look it's just … just sometimes … sometimes we get … we just get a bit on each other's nerves.
	Doesn't mean … mean anything … that's *all* it is.
	Pause.
	That's all it is.
	Pause.
	Cheer up. Tell you what, we'll try out that boomerang Grandad's given you.
BEN:	When?
BOB:	About an hour? I'll make us a picnic.
BEN:	*(Quite excitedly.)* Will Grandad come with us?
BOB:	'Course he will. 'Course he will.
	Blackout.

Lights up. The park. Midday.

BEN, BOB and GRANDAD *appear.*

BEN *carries a boomerang, suggested.*

BOB *carries sandwiches in a plastic bag.*

BEN *looks around, clearly very frustrated, wanting badly to throw the boomerang.*

BOB: How'd it go at the doctor's?

GRANDAD: OK … fine.

BOB: So everything's ok?

GRANDAD: No problem.

BOB: Good. What was causing the pain, then?

GRANDAD: Something or nothing. Just do me a favour now? Give it a rest?

BOB: I was just a bit worried.

GRANDAD: There's no need to be. He's given me some antibiotics.

Pause.

BEN: *(Shouts.) Here* then, Grandad?

GRANDAD: Too near those trees.

BOB: Don't believe this.

BEN: Dad, can I throw it now?

BOB: *Wait!*

GRANDAD: I should go somewhere else with it. Go somewhere else.

Somewhere open. *Open.* Go where there's no trees.

BOB: There's nowhere.

GRANDAD: There must be.

BOB: *(Emphatically.)* There's nowhere near here.

GRANDAD: *(Sighs, dismissively.)* Alright. Let him throw it. Don't listen to me. Since when have you ever listened to me?

BOB: Dad, we're nowhere near the trees. *Nowhere* near.

GRANDAD: Let him throw it, then.

BEN: Can I, dad?

BOB: *(Firmly.) Wait!*

            Pause.

GRANDAD: They're pine trees. Look at 'em. No climbing *them.* If it gets stuck in one, he can kiss it goodbye. Look how high they are. Look at 'em. Nothing to grip.

            Pause.

            Straight as a dye.

            Pause.

BEN: Dad.

BOB: What?

BEN: *Can* we go somewhere else?

BOB: Like where?

BEN: Somewhere else. Go where there's no trees.

GRANDAD: Queens Common.

BOB: *(Incredulously.)* Queens Common?

GRANDAD: That's the best bet. Come on. Plenty wide open spaces …

BOB: Miles away!

GRANDAD: No! We'll be there in twenty minutes.

BEN: Dad, can we go? Can we go to Queens Common, dad?

BOB: *(Very firm.)* NO!

Pause.

BEN *sulks.*

GRANDAD *takes out his pipe, starts to fill it.*

BOB: (*Relents.*) Look, throw it. *Low.* Try throwing it low.

GRANDAD: If he throws it, he'll lose it.

BOB: It's safe enough here.

GRANDAD: (*Chuckles.*) Throw it low?

BOB: Go on, Ben.

GRANDAD: A boomerang rises.

BOB: (*Commands.*) Throw it.

GRANDAD: Rises. Rises and curls.

BOB: Are you throwing it or not? Or shall we go home?

BEN: I don't want to lose it.

BOB: (*Turns on* GRANDAD.) See what you've done?

GRANDAD: What have *I* done?

BOB: Throw it, Ben!

GRANDAD: Leave me out of it.

BOB: (*Pained.*) *Why* did you give it him?

GRANDAD: Just leave me out.

BOB: Now he's too scared to throw it.

BEN: I don't want to lose it.

BOB: Throw it low. Give it here. Watch me throw it. Watch *me* throw it. *Watch.*

BOB *throws boomerang.* ALL THREE *watch its journey through the sky.*

BEN: Wow! Watch it curl!

BOB: (*Suddenly worried.*) Oh ... (*Soft groan.*) No ...
(*Groans loudly, covers face with hands.*) NO!

GRANDAD: (*Slowly, all knowing.*) What did I say?

Silence.

BOB *looks up, slowly.*

ALL THREE *stare at the boomerang, now stuck high in a tree.*

BOB *slowly at first, taking careful aim, now begins to throw stones to dislodge the boomerang.*

BEN *sits on bench, sulking.*

GRANDAD *puffs his pipe, occasionally shaking his head.*

Throughout the following dialogue, BOB*'s stone throwing becomes increasingly frantic.*

GRANDAD: I knew this would happen. Foregone conclusion.

(Wearily.) What did I tell you, Bob? What did I say?

Would you listen, eh? No chance.

(Small chuckle.) Listen to me?

Pause.

No chance of that.

Pause.

Forget it. You've lost it. The boomerang's lost.

You've lost it. Pack it in. Pack it in now.

You've no chance. Forget it. You've lost it for good.

Pause.

It's up there for good.

Pause.

BOB *throws off his jacket, continues throwing stones.*

He is panting quite heavily, his face flushed.

It's funny how people stare a mess in the face and still run headlong into it. *(Sighs.)* Yes … it's funny how some people never seem to learn.

(Great sigh.) Still … takes all sorts …

Pause.

BEN: Grandad?

GRANDAD: Eh?

BEN: If dad can't get it down …

GRANDAD: Oh he won't get it down, son.

BEN: If … if he can't …

GRANDAD: He can throw stones all day 'till he's blue in the face.

            No … he won't get it down.

            Pause.

            BOB *moves around, starts to throw stones from a different angle.*

BEN: Will I be able to buy another one like it, Grandad?

GRANDAD: I'm afraid you won't.

BEN: Why not?

GRANDAD: They don't make 'em like that anymore. No. Not any more. No. Like I said, it was given to my father by an old aborigine a long time ago.

            My father had saved the aborigine's life.

BEN: Saved his life?

GRANDAD: I told you.

BEN: No. No, you didn't.

GRANDAD: I'm sure I did.

BEN: No, Grandad.

GRANDAD: Thought I had.

BEN: No.

GRANDAD: Well, you've heard of cow disease? Mad cow disease?

            It was on last night's news. You saw it.

BEN: Yeah.

GRANDAD: Well, there's also such a thing as mad kangaroo disease.

	Didn't know that, did you?
BEN:	No.
GRANDAD:	Oh yes. When my father went out there fifty years ago, Australia was plagued with mad kangaroos.
BEN:	Were they all mad?
GRANDAD:	Nutters. All stark raving mad.
BEN:	What? *All* of them?
GRANDAD:	No … well, some of them were sane.
	But the kangaroo which charged at the aborigine was definitely two bricks short of a load. It just charged straight at him. My father pushed him out of the way in the nick of time and saved him from wearing a wooden overcoat.
BEN:	*(Impressed.)* Saved his life, eh?
GRANDAD:	Saved his life. So the aborigine was so very grateful he gave my father his best boomerang.
	Then my father handed it down to me.
	And I, in turn, handed it down to you.
BEN:	But why did you not hand it down to dad, first?
GRANDAD:	Because I knew *he'd* bloody well lose it!
	BOB *throws stones at greater intervals, now, glaring with venom, up at the tree.*
GRANDAD:	He was always losing things as a boy.
	All his life he's lost things. All his life.
	(Shouts to BOB.*)* Pack it in!
BOB:	I've moved it.
GRANDAD:	Moved it, my eye.
BOB:	I've moved it.
GRANDAD:	Half an inch?
BOB:	More than that.
GRANDAD:	No.

BOB: (*Panting.*) Keep on hitting it …

GRANDAD: *No* chance.

BOB: Each time I hit it, it moves.

GRANDAD: You're imagining things.

BOB: (*With certainty.*) No, I'm not.

GRANDAD: Look, those branches are holding it just like a vice. It's stuck in that tree for good.

            Pause.

BOB: (*Breezily, puts on a brave face.*) Let's have a sandwich. Let's have some lunch.

            Don't worry about it. I'll get it down, Ben.

            Just a question of hitting it in the right place.

            Come on, now, let's have a bite.

            Pause.

            BOB *hands out sandwiches.*

            GRANDAD & BOB *eat.*

            BEN *stares at his sandwiches, glum.*

            BOB *takes out soft drinks, hands one to* BEN.

            BEN *holds the drink, stares at it, glum.*

BOB: Come on, Ben. Eat up, then.

BEN: Not hungry.

BOB: Come on.

            Pause.

            Got some nice biscuits for afters.

            Pause.

            Nice biscuits. Your favourites. *Chocolate Meringues.*

            Eat up, now. There's a good lad.

            Pause.

            Look, I know you're fed up. I'm fed up as well.

            I'm trying my best to get it down. If I *can't* get it

down, I'll buy you another. Another one like it.
Fair? Fair enough? Can't say fairer than that, now.
Can I, now? Eh?

Pause.

Can't say fairer than that.

Pause.

BEN: You can't buy another one.

BOB: Sorry?

BEN: You can't. You can't buy another one like it.

Pause.

BOB: Not *exactly* like it. Not *quite* the same...

BEN: It was special.

BOB: Special?

BEN: Different.

BOB: How? How different?

BEN: It had been handed down.

BOB: Eh?

BEN: Handed down.

BOB: Handed down?

BEN: Can't buy it in shops.

Dad, they just don't make them like that anymore.

BOB: *(Exasperated.)* Anybody would think I've lost the Crown Jewels!

(Stern.) Eat up. Come on. Eat your sandwich.

Pause.

BOB & GRANDAD *eat.*

BEN *sits, sulking.*

GRANDAD *starts to whistle,* 'Keep The Home Fires Burning'. *The whistling continues for some time then stops.*

BOB *eating sandwich, gets to his feet, stands, stares up at the tree.*

BOB: I'll borrow a ladder. That's what I'll do. Just need a ladder.

That's all I need. That ladder of yours, dad, will fit the bill fine.

GRANDAD: Look, forget it, eh? Please? You'll break your neck.

I'm telling you, you'll break your bloody neck.

You're no good on ladders. You know that, yourself.

BOB: I'll be careful.

BEN: Dad. Can I have a meringue?

BOB: No, you can't.

BEN: Why not?

BOB: Eat your sandwich. Come on. Eat your sandwich.

BEN: I've eaten it.

BOB: You're lying. Don't lie. No sandwich—no chocolate meringue.

Pause.

GRANDAD: If you fall off that ladder, *then* what will you do?

If you're laid off work? No money, eh? Well?

BOB: Wouldn't make much difference, as it happens…

GRANDAD: Eh?

BOB: I'll be out of work anyway. Couple of weeks.

GRANDAD: Out of work? Out of work?

BOB: Oh, haven't you heard? They're making yours truly redundant.

GRANDAD: What?

BEN: Dad, I've finished my sandwich.

BOB: Can't have.

BEN: I *have.*

BOB: You're lying.

BEN: I've finished it.

BOB: Don't bloody lie!

GRANDAD: Oh leave him. Leave him. Leave him alone. If he wants to starve, let him.

BOB: He's telling me lies.

GRANDAD: *Let* him starve.

BOB: *(Grabs* BEN*, shakes him.)* He's telling me thundering great lies!

BEN: *(Struggling free, runs off.)* Let go of me! Leave me alone!

BOB: *(Shouts.)* Come back! Do you hear me? Come back *now!*

            BOB, GRANDAD *stand a moment.*

            BOB a*ngrily throws a stone up at the tree.*

            He throws a second stone.

            He turns away, stands, his back to GRANDAD.

            Pause.

BOB: *(Softly.)* Go and get him.

GRANDAD: Leave him. Leave him a while.

BOB: He's upset.

GRANDAD: Just leave him.

BOB: *(Turns, looks out.)* Where is he?

GRANDAD: *(Points.)* There.

BOB: Can't see him.

GRANDAD: He's sulking. Down by the swings.

BOB: Go and get him.

GRANDAD: He'll come when he's ready.

            Pause.

            When did you hear...about the job?

BOB: Last week.

GRANDAD: How many are they laying off?

BOB: Half.

GRANDAD: *(Shocked.)* Half the workforce?

BOB: They're closing down half the plant.

GRANDAD: Oh God.

BOB: He won't help.

GRANDAD: What will you do?

BOB: What would *you* do?

GRANDAD: Dunno ...

BOB: *I* don't bloody know.

GRANDAD: Retrain?

BOB: Retrain? Retrain for what? There's nothing else round here.

          There're no other jobs. There's nothing here. Nothing.

          Retrain, he says. Great.

          Pause.

          Tell me the point.

          Pause.

          You were right.

GRANDAD: What about?

BOB: Me losing things.

          Pause.

          All my life.

          Pause.

          All my sodding life.

          Pause.

          First my business. My house. My house and my car. Now I'm even losing this stupid job.

Tell me, what have I left, eh? What have I left?

GRANDAD: You've your life.

BOB: My life? My life's like *that!*

Like that stupid boomerang! Stuck up a tree!

GRANDAD: You've *time.*

BOB: Time?

GRANDAD: Still got time on your side.

BOB: That right?

GRANDAD: My time's run out.

Pause.

BOB: Run out?

Pause.

How do you mean?

Pause.

How do you mean? Run out?

Pause.

What you on about? What you on about, eh?

How do you mean? Run out?

Pause.

You've just seen the doc. Haven't you just seen the doc?

The doctor's given you a clean bill of health.

GRANDAD: Yes, I know ...

BOB: So how come ...?

GRANDAD: Time's *running* out. I should have said *running* out.

BOB: Different thing!

GRANDAD: Even so, things seem a bit different lately.

Little things I'm seeing ... didn't see before.

Oh, I saw them. 'Course I did. Flowers ... birds ...

I saw them. They're *there*. They've always been there.

I just didn't … didn't look at them. Didn't *really* look.

I didn't really *see* them. Know what I mean? No, you don't. You don't know. Don't know, do you?

BOB: I think I do.

GRANDAD: No … you don't.

Pause.

BEN: *(reappears.)* Can we go?

Pause.

We'll be late for the match.

Pause.

Dad? Can we go?

Pause.

GRANDAD: He's right. We'll be late. Early kick-off today.

Two-thirty kick-off. We'd best be off now.

BOB: What about the boomerang?

GRANDAD: Leave it. It's lost.

BOB: I'll come back tomorrow.

GRANDAD: Shouldn't bother.

BOB: I will. I'll come back with a ladder.

GRANDAD: Let's be off, eh?

BOB: I'll get it down.

GRANDAD: Ready? Let's go.

GRANDAD & BEN *go off.*

BOB *stands, stares up at the boomerang a moment.*

He turns, follows them.

Blackout.

Noise of football match crowd.

Spotlight snaps on.

In spotlight, BOB, GRANDAD *and* BEN *watch the match.*

ALL THREE wear black and white scarves.

GRANDAD: Offside!

BOB: A mile off!

GRANDAD: Wake up!

BOB: Come on!

GRANDAD: Wake up ref, for Godsake!

BEN: Useless!

BOB: Come on! Down your wing! *Down your wing!*

GRANDAD: That's better.

BOB: Good ball!

BEN: In the middle!

BOB: Through ball!

GRANDAD: On his own!

ALL THREE: *SHOOT!*

GRANDAD: *(Groans.)* Oh for Godsake.

BOB: He'll lose it.

GRANDAD: Shoot you fool!

ALL THREE: *SHOOT!*

BOB: Too bloody slow.

BEN: Corner!

BOB: Come on, now! *Come on!*

ALL THREE: *(Chant.)* TWO! FOUR! SIX! EIGHT!

WHO DO WE APPREC ... CI ... ATE?!

BOB: Chance to draw level.

GRANDAD: *Last* chance, this.

BOB: How long we got?

GRANDAD: Seconds.

BOB: Come on! Make it count! *(Groans.)* Oh no.

Don't believe it! He's put it behind!

That's it. Lost again, eh? One nil again.

(Angrily.) We missed *three* good chances.

One open goal. How he missed that, I don't know.

(Shouts after players.) Right lot of dickheads!
Couldn't win a one ticket raffle!

Blackout.

Lights up. Kitchen. Night.

BEN *sits, writing letter. He finishes writing, reads letter.*

BEN'S VOICEOVER: Dear mum, I hope you'll soon feel better in Blackpool.

Dad says you need a good rest. I'm sorry you're tired, mum.

When you come home, I promise I'll try not to make you more tired. I'll work harder at school and do all my homework. You won't have to nag me. Ever again. I'll do just as you tell me. Well, most of the time ...

Please come home soon, mum. Miss you. Love, Ben.

PS. Can you bring me some Blackpool Rock?

BEN *nods, pleased with letter, puts letter in envelope.*

He licks and seals envelope.

BOB: *(Enters.)* What you got there?

BEN: A letter. A letter for mum. Can you post it to Auntie Pat's?

BOB: Give it here, then.

BEN: *(Hands him letter.)* When's she coming back?

BOB: Oh ... she shouldn't be long, now.

BEN: How long? 'bout a week?

BOB: A bit longer than that.

BEN: Is she *so* tired?

BOB:	She's … she's very run down.
BEN:	Run down?
BOB:	She just … just needs a good rest.
BEN:	She'll be well soon?
BOB:	'Course she will. 'Course she will. 'Course. Go to bed, now.
BEN:	'Night dad.
BOB:	Night.

BEN goes off.

Pause.

BOB stands a moment.

He stares at the letter, opens it, reads.

He screws up the letter, slowly sits, slumped.

He starts to sob, quietly, head in hand.

Fade.

Lights up. Kitchen. Morning.

BOB & GRANDAD sit, sipping tea from mugs.

A bag of apples is on the table, next to GRANDAD.

Pause.

They both sip their tea.

GRANDAD: Anne out again?

BOB: Yeah.

GRANDAD: She's always out. Gone shopping?

BOB: No. She's away for a bit. Gone to Blackpool. She needed a bit of a rest. She's been overdoing it.

          Working too hard.

GRANDAD: She's a wonderful girl. A first class wife. She's a diamond.

          Just like your mum, rest her soul. I've said it before and

          I'll say it again. She's worth her weight in gold.

          Pause.

          When's she coming back, then?

BOB: She shouldn't be long. When she's better. When she feels better.

          Pause.

GRANDAD: Blackpool, eh?

          (Fondly.) Blackpool sands.

          Pause.

          The old golden mile.

          Pause.

A long time since we went there. A lifetime ago.

Last time we went there you were wearing short pants.

Yes, the old golden mile. Used to love it, you did.

The amusement stalls. Couldn't keep you away.

There was one ... an *old* stall ... your favourite, it was ... what was it ...?

The boxers. The boxers, that's right. Boxers stood in a circle.

A ball on a chain. The ball hit a wheel. A revolving wheel.

The ball hit a wheel, knocked each boxer down.

If yours was left up at the end, then you won.

(Small chuckle.) But the only trouble was, you never *did* win.

Your boxer was always knocked down first! Whichever you picked.

Joe Louis ... didn't matter ... Jersey Joe Walcott ... Freddy Mills ...

Even Rocky Marciano. *(Laughs.)* Crash bang wallop!

Flat on their bloody backs!

Pause.

Well, since Ann's not here, it's a good time to ask you about her birthday.

BOB: Birthday?

GRANDAD: Next week.

BOB: Oh yeah.

GRANDAD: *(Incredulously)* You'd forgotten! You'd forgotten!

BOB: I hadn't.

GRANDAD: You could have fooled me, son. Could have fooled me.

Well, anyway, have you any ideas about what she'd like as a present?

BOB: Dunno …

GRANDAD: Would she like a bracelet?

BOB: Bracelet? Dunno …

GRANDAD: Or a brooch? How about a nice brooch?

Pause.

Well, think on it, will you? Give it some thought.

I'll need to know in the next couple of days.

(Casually.) By the way, I've gone and booked us a meal.

BOB: A meal?

GRANDAD: For her birthday. At *The Pack Horse*. I've booked us a table.

Table for four.

(BOB frowns.)

Well, I thought you'd be pleased.

BOB: I am. I am. It's just that …

GRANDAD: What?

BOB: That'll set you back, won't it?

GRANDAD: *My* money, son. Let me worry about that.

BOB: *The Pack Horse*? What happened? You came up on the pools?

GRANDAD: I just thought I'd give her a special treat.

It's her fortieth, isn't it? Fortieth? Right?

BOB: Dad, there's something I think … I think I should … well … there's something I think you should … think you should know …

GRANDAD: She's gone vegetarian?

BOB: No, it's not that …

GRANDAD: What is it, then?

BOB: It ... it's just that she ...

GRANDAD: What?

BOB: It's just that she ...

GRANDAD: *(Slightly impatient.)* Bob ...

BOB: Forget it. Alright?

GRANDAD: What you saying? What is it you're trying to say?

BOB: Nothing.

GRANDAD: Next Friday it is, then.

          Blackout.

Lights up. Kitchen. Late Morning.

BEN *sits at the table. He opens a letter, reads.*

ANNE'S VOICEOVER: Dear Ben, it's hard to write this letter.

I didn't want to write it at all, but I must.

Ben, your dad and me, we haven't been happy.

We're just not happy together anymore.

It's nobody's fault. Please try and understand.

People fall in love … they can fall out of love.

Ben, your dad and me, we've just grown apart.

I'm sorry. Sorry it's turned out this way but it's better for now if you stay in England and finish your schooling. Do well at school and, who knows?

You might get a job here in Spain!

I'll write again soon. Ben.

All my love, Mum.

BOB *enters, looks around, looking slightly puzzled.*

BEN *quickly puts letter away.)*

BOB: No mail come today, Ben?

BEN: No.

BOB: That's strange. I thought I just heard the postman.

No? Oh, well… well, no news is good news.

That's what they say.

Pause.

That's what they say.

Pause.

What do you fancy doing today? Do you fancy fishing?

How about fishing? We could go down to Brooklands.

They've stocked it with trout. Someone told me last week that it's choc-full of trout.

Pause.

What do you say?

Pause.

No, perhaps not. Our permit's expired.

I'll have to renew it. Expired last month.

That'll cost me. Cost me an arm and a leg.

Come on. Eat up. Eat your toast.

Pause.

Tell you what, we'll borrow Grandad's ladder and get that bloody boomerang down.

No time like the present, eh? That's what we'll do.

We'll show Grandad, eh? We'll get it down, right?

We'll show him, eh? Shall we? Killjoy, he is.

He's so sure we've lost it.

(Imitates GRANDAD's *voice.)* It's up there for good.

Those branches are holding it just like a vice!

(Own voice.) Eat up. I'll go, get the ladder now, eh?

I'll be back in ten minutes. Eat up.

BOB *goes out.*

Silence.

BEN *stares ahead.*

Blackout.

Lights up. The Park. Morning.

BOB, GRANDAD and BEN are looking up at the tree and ladder which are both suggested, off left.

BEN holds a soft drinks can.

BOB is panting, quite heavily, his face very flushed.

GRANDAD: *(To BOB.)* What did I tell you? What did I say?

The ladder's not long enough. Not by a mile.

(Incredulously, small chuckle, points.) How did you ever imagine you'd reach it on *that?*

(Sighs, shakes head.) Dear oh dear oh dear...

BOB turns away from GRANDAD, slumps down on the bench.

Pause.

BEN drinks.

GRANDAD: *(Turns to BEN.)* That's it. Come on, now. Drink your drink.

Pause.

Drink your drink.

Pause.

Come on, Ben. Cheer up. Cheer up, now. Come on.

Pause.

Not the end of the world.

Pause.

I think it's his mum. He's missing his mum.

Not the boomerang so much, is it, now? No.

He's missing her dinners. Yes, *that's what it is.*

Cheer up. She'll soon be back.

Pause.

It's her birthday next week. Have you bought her a present?

What did you get for her? What did you get?

(Turns away.) Oh, I see. Top secret? *Top secret's top secret.*

Ok mate, I understand.

Pause.

By the way, on her birthday … your dad might have told you … I'm taking you all out to *The Pack Horse*. I'm taking you all for a big slap-up meal.

I'm…

Sudden groan from GRANDAD.

BOB: *(Stands.)* Dad?

GRANDAD: *(Gasps for breath.)* It's alright. Alright.

BOB: What's wrong?

GRANDAD: It'll go … just a pain, it …

BOB: Dad …

GRANDAD: *(Shouts through his pain.)* It's *alright*! Just leave me!

Leave me! Leave me alone!

Pause.

(Gasps, softly.) Leave me alone.

Blackout.

Lights up. Wing chair. Evening.

GRANDAD *sits in the wing chair, asleep.*

BOB & BEN *stand by his side.*

BOB: Let him sleep, Ben. There's no point waking him up.

Pause.

Let him sleep.

Pause.

He's in the best place. This hospice is the best.

Pause.

They'll look after him, here.

Pause.

You know what our trouble was? Your Grandad and me?

We couldn't … couldn't really … really … talk.

Oh we'd talk about football, cricket and stuff, but we couldn't … couldn't really … *(Breaks off.)*

Pause.

We talk though, don't we? I always said if I had a son of my own, we'd talk. And we *do* talk, don't we?

Of course we do.

Pause.

We talk all the time.

Pause.

Did I ever tell you that you have your mum's eyes?

When we were younger … falling in love.

Did I ever say you look like she did then?

BEN: No.

BOB: Well ... you do.

Fade.